Promoting learning

Kate Malone

Published by the National Institute of
Adult Continuing Education (England and Wales)

21 De Montfort Street
Leicester LE1 7GE
Company registration no. 2603322
Charity registration no. 1002775

First published 2003

The *NIACE lifelines in adult learning series* is supported by the Adult
and Community Learning Fund. ACLF is funded by the Department
for Education and Skills and managed in partnership by NIACE and
the Basic Skills Agency to develop widening participation in adult learning.

promoting adult learning

NIACE has a broad remit to promote lifelong learning
opportunities for adults. NIACE works to develop
increased participation in education and training,
particularly for those who do not have easy access
because of barriers of class, gender, age, race,
language and culture, learning difficulties and
disabilities, or insufficient financial resources.

www.niace.org.uk

Cataloguing in Publication Data
A CIP record of this title is available from the British Library

Designed and typeset by Boldface
Printed in Great Britain by Russell Press, Nottingham

ISBN 1 86201 152 4

Contents

Note to the reader

Inspirations: refer to case studies and examples of good practice.
Glossary: the meanings of the words underlined in the text can be found in the glossary on page 34.

1 Recognising the issue

We are a society where nine in ten of us believe that learning makes a positive difference to our work chances, to the quality of our lives and to our children's prospects. Yet one in four of us still acts as though learning is not for the likes of us.

While the overall number of adults participating in organised learning has grown over the last decade, their social composition has remained stubbornly resistant to change. A third of all adults still do not take part in any learning activity. With the advent of the communications age, people who are not tuning in are likely to be left out. In 2002, the annual NIACE survey into participation patterns showed that participation in learning is much higher among middle-class groups rather than working-class groups; younger people rather than older people; men rather than women; and people in work rather than those who are not economically active. In addition, participation in learning is much more likely when people have access to the Internet.

The increased emphasis on lifelong learning in recent years and additional resources made available to encourage preparation for and participation in the knowledge economy means that there are now many centres which provide IT training, and access to the Internet, free of charge. Just as there are many which provide basic skills training free of charge, and many which provide exactly the opportunities which can be the catalyst to change lives.

As surveys over the years have shown, the people who should be making the most of these opportunities are still hard to reach and hard to engage. This has just as much to do with the various barriers set up by educational and training institutions as with feelings of alienation or lack of confidence among prospective learners. Many people do not know what opportunities exist and frequently do not imagine that education has much to offer them. For those who are more aware that learning matters, the barriers to participation and success can still seem enormous.

2 Why a campaign

When your target audience is adults who have been out of learning for some time you need to do more than produce a prospectus and hope they'll come rushing in. Adults have different needs and many things will discourage them from starting something new. They 'juggle' many roles and responsibilities. The existing patterns of their lives can seem to give little extra time for additional learning.

Adults are most likely to be attracted to learn in places where they feel comfortable already. They need to be encouraged into learning by something which is both relevant to them and which adds something positive to their lives.

A campaign can offer the mixture of celebration and awareness-raising elements that helps to awaken someone's motivation to learn. Adult Learners' Week, for example, is a national campaign led by NIACE, concerned with promoting learning as widely as possible. In preparation for the annual week of events and awards and media coverage, we flood local newspapers and radio with examples of real people who have positive stories to tell, in the hope of encouraging the "*if they can do it, so can I*" principle. So long as the story is not too extraordinary, listeners and readers often start to see themselves doing something similar.

Specific campaigns can also be a highly effective way of promoting learning on a more local basis. Campaigns are not the same thing as ongoing policies and provision for learning. They are essentially strategies to publicise and promote activities, to raise awareness and to encourage people to get involved. A campaigning approach to recruitment and awareness-raising suggests a lively and pro-active attitude on the part of learning providers – whether they are large institutions such as colleges or small voluntary and community organisations.

3 Getting started

Organisers often approach the mechanics of a campaign differently, but there are is set of key elements. Here a dramatised case study shows how the various elements are related:

Who do you want to reach and why?

A voluntary sector organisation in London was aware that the local (large) population of migrant workers had poor records of education, few qualifications, and low awareness of local education initiatives. These were all factors that were holding them back from improving their English skills, helping with their children's homework and their own career progression. Often these were families that were living in near-poverty and exhibiting higher levels of ill health and social isolation than other people in the area.

What do you want to do?

The organisation decided to run a publicity campaign to raise awareness among the migrant community of the existence of cheap, local, high-quality provision. They wanted to persuade people it was a good idea to learn and to take advantage of the provision.

How do you go about it?

The group organised a mailshot that targeted the homes of migrant workers and the restaurants, hospitals and hotels where they worked. Because they had a good knowledge of local need, they knew that people may be uncomfortable learning in very formal venues. So they invited local providers to give talks and "tasters" of learning in the community centre. They asked a local radio station to give details of the taster sessions and use real-life learners to talk on-air about their own experiences.

Sponsorship

The group persuaded a local company to print the mailshot leaflets free of charge. They received financial support from the European Social Fund to help pay for other publicity and for the hire of the community centre. They persuaded local tutors to give their time free of charge.

Outcome

The group found that many of the people who had seen a leaflet, heard something on the radio or attended one of the community-based taster sessions expressed an interest in signing up to a longer course. The participants had made the connection between learning and "getting on". They realised that some of the problems they thought existed, for example, not having enough money to learn, not being able to speak English or having nowhere to keep their children occupied, could be easily solved.

Progression

The organisation secured extra funding to offer an advice centre in the community centre, where people could ask in a friendly, familiar environment about different courses and how to pay for them. Eventually they were able to secure enough funding to run IT classes in the centre, free of charge.

The key points from this case study are:

- knowing in advance what the local needs and issues are;
- defining clear objectives;
- designing a campaign aimed directly at the target audience;
- creating publicity that is sent or placed in settings where the target group lives, works or visits, and in a format which is relevant;
- taking advantage of agencies who may already be working with prospective adult learners but offering different opportunities (ie. the tutors).

If some or all of this sounds familiar – read on for further advice about promoting learning.

4 Planning a campaign

In order to start thinking about promoting the learning you are offering you will need to consider the following:

- knowing who you want to reach – and why;
- proper consultation;
- working with partners;
- planning;
- publicity – including research, the media and promotional material;
- sponsorship;
- evaluating the outcome.

SELF DEFENCE CLASS, WEA DONCASTER © BARRY JOHNSON PHOTOGRAPHY

5 Knowing who you want to reach – and why

When you are planning promotional events, it's important to decide who you want to target and get to know them. Decide whether the group in question means people living in a geographical area, new learners or existing learners, the media or other organisations or decision-makers. Knowing your target group should then help you to decide your next step – how to target them and by what means.

Start by asking the people who are most likely to know what will work. This means doing some research about organisations who have already made links with the target group and are trying to involve them. When planning your promotional activities it is strongly recommended that you also involve members of the target group in all your discussions (see below and also Lifeline 5: *Consulting Adults*).

Reaching those sections of the community who are the most difficult to reach or who are turned off by traditional images of learning presents the most challenging task for campaign organisers. How can you break down the barriers and capture their imagination? The message you are delivering must be relevant, appropriate, friendly and inspiring.

Alternatively, you may want to raise awareness of the issues facing learners among those who make or contribute toward decisions. An audience in this instance might consist of training organisations, councils, businesses, community or religious leaders, policy-makers or politicians. Community organisations and local activists will want to see how your ideas can benefit the greater community. Business leaders will be interested in the economic benefits to their organisations.

If your objective is to widen participation, you will be targeting groups who are under-represented. For example:

- people who are unemployed might want learning to help them gain confidence and new skills;
- workers may want to improve their wages and standard of living;
- retired people may want to enjoy new hobbies or make new friends;
- citizens may want to get more involved in local community concerns.

During Adult Learners' Week, a motivational message about the Week is printed on over one million giro slips encouraging people in receipt of unemployment benefits to ring learndirect and find out what opportunities are available.

A REVIEW OF
ADULT LEARNERS' WEEK
19-25 MAY 1997

16-22 May 1998
Adult Learners' Week

6 Consultation and involvement

Research has shown that the majority of adults find out about learning opportunities through the workplace or through their friends and peers. These are the most fruitful contexts in which to plan and implement your campaigns. See learners as promoters but making sure that you support their efforts.

There are no better experts on people than people themselves. And there are no better advocates and evangelists about the benefits of learning than those who have experienced learning for themselves. Adult learners should be consulted and included at every stage of the campaign process, from initial research through to providing stories for the media; from helping run the activity to recording outcomes.

Involving existing learners from the outset helps to tell the story of how people's lives are enriched and transformed by discovering talents and skills and by gaining in confidence and self-worth. It is a chance for potential learners to hear about other people's experiences, for tutors to remind themselves why they do the job they do, and for stakeholders to be reminded of the importance of true community learning.

Ten practical tips for involving learners

We asked NIACE'S Adult Learners' Forum for some advice about this. These are their questions and recommendations:

- It is better to invite two or more learners to take part in the activities being planned. This allows for flexibility in attendance and also they can provide mutual support.
- It is essential to ensure that travel or related expenses are available in advance. Learners cannot be expected to find money for travel or subsistence.
- Childcare costs need to be offered and met and an understanding needs to made clear at the beginning.
- Don't always rely on the same two or three people – learners move on. A process whereby different learners are involved should be put in place.
- If a learner loses a day's pay by attending your activity, compensation for the pay should be covered. When professionals attend activities they usually do so as part of their paid job.
- A representative from the relevant organisation should be allocated to 'look

after' the learners so they have a point of contact and can take the time to fill in any background and jargon that may arise.

- Consideration needs to be given to the timing of activities. Are activities easy to get to? Is the timing appropriate for people with children who have to travel a fair distance?
- What is the purpose of the learner's presence at the activities? If they are there to play an equal role to that of the professionals, ensure other members of the group use as little jargon as possible and behave in a way that does not patronise.
- Learners will come with passion and commitment to do a 'job'. If they see that their enthusiasm is not being used they will be disappointed and stop attending. There must be commitment on both sides to make it work.
- The learner might benefit from training prior to their involvement. Is your organisation willing to cover the cost of this training?

7 Working with partners

Building effective partnerships is key to all good promotional activities. Successful initiatives work closely with other relevant agencies to ensure that local resources are used in the most effective way. Pooling resources also opens the door to more opportunities for potential learners to get involved in. Partnerships engage a wider range of people, enable a bigger choice of activities, pool the experiences of specialists, and set on the table the concerns of adult learners from different backgrounds.

There is benefit in developing links with existing groups of various kinds – local communities and structures such as Parish and District Councils; informal gatherings such as pub regulars or users of leisure/sports clubs; parents of children at local schools or playgroups; and work communities.

Partnership working can benefit organisations by:

- equipping people within the partnership with new skills;
- creating opportunities for creativity, collaboration and understanding of different organisational strengths and cultures;
- enabling new learners to be reached.

The attributes of a good partner

A good partner has:

- a defined role;
- the same goals (agreed at the outset);
- their own autonomy;
- expertise or resources to offer and is clear about their contribution;
- a commitment to working as part of a team of organisations;
- the ability and commitment to build solid relationships and trust;
- the capability of delivering what has been agreed.

Putting good partners together creates an effective partnership, which will:

- focus on the target group and its needs;
- involve the organisations necessary to reach those target groups;
- agree on a strategy and have clear objectives and a common aim;

- use partners' strengths, skills, experience and knowledge to work more effectively;
- offer time and commitment to actively get involved;
- understand each member's specific role and responsibilities;
- share visions/interests/common outcomes;
- offer a clear decision-making process and good communication;
- get enjoyment from working together.

The Newspapers in Education Project is a unique partnership between the *Newcastle Chronicle & Journal* Ltd, Telewest Business, the local education authority and communities across the North East. The project supports the education and development of the people of the North East, introducing them to the world of media and the benefits of more effective communication while improving lifelong learning across the region. The learning centre offers courses, access to media journalism, materials to support trainers and teachers, insight into the media industry, teacher training and open days with full-time staffing.

MIND and the Adult Education Service in North Humberside joined forces to run a one-day 'Creative Minds' showcase in the town hall. The celebration showed the creativity of people with mental illness and provided a positive presentation of people who have left long-stay hospitals to live in the community.

The Spring into Learning Festival was co-ordinated by the Greater Nottingham Learning Partnership, which produced 14,000 copies of a calendar detailing more than 100 events. As part of the festival, ten market stalls staffed by providers from college, careers service and other volunteers provided information about the availability of courses, as well as general advice and guidance.

Don't forget that there needs to be clear commitment from all partners to share knowledge and expertise. Clear roles and responsibilities should be established at the outset. Meeting your partners at regular intervals to share information means that no-one will be left out of discussions and everyone will have a chance to contribute.

8 Planning the event

Choose your activity

The community education department in Peterborough found that there were few men, especially young ones, coming forward to take advantage of learning opportunities in the area. Existing classes weren't attracting them. What was needed was a new look at how the learning was presented.

The organisers re-located some laptop computers to the Peter Pan, a regulars' pub on a local council estate. Software was offered that would be appealing to men, along with advice sessions. The laptops acted as an incentive and attracted men to receive information and guidance about further learning opportunities.

The activity depended on a good partnership between the careers service, the local main library and the landlord of the pub. The cleverness of this campaign was the insight into where the target audience felt most at ease, and the ability to identify learning activities that matched their interests. The moral is if you want to reach non-traditional learners, you should look at non-traditional venues and events.

Use an element of theatre to fire the imagination, interrupt daily activity and create space for something unexpected or new. If people can be engaged for even a short time doing something different, this may provide an opportunity to plant the seeds of possibility and the potential for change.

There are definite benefits in local knowledge and planning – knowing what will go on the patch and having a feel for local needs and interests. But there are also dangers – in particular offering 'more of the same' and attracting people who are already persuaded of the value of learning and aware of what is available. There is a need to combine local planning with overall co-ordination and cross-fertilisation of a proactive kind. This means a combination of both 'tried and tested' and experimental activities and opportunities, and a range of activities designed to appeal to a wider range of interests and potential learning styles and purposes.

Activities to promote learning can range from tasters to performances. Some of the many possibilities are listed below:

- tasters or 'have a go' sessions;
- open days;
- bring-a-friend sessions;
- celebrations or award ceremonies;

SPIRATIONS

In Lichfield, shoppers at Do-It-All were encouraged to have a go at a variety of activities, including clay modelling.

Derby City of Learning organised learning 'tasters' in two community centres in a multi-cultural inner-city area. Both were within walking distance of each other, but transport was laid on for people with mobility problems. Regulars and visitors were introduced to learning and training opportunities across Derby as well as offered information in areas such as health, cultural issues, and the voluntary sector. The event also helped increase the knowledge of potential learners by addressing individual needs in a culturally sensitive manner.

The WEA organised learning opportunities for residents of an old people's home. The residential guest-house in Norfolk lent out a room for classes while tutors were arranged by the WEA. Because not all of the residents were able to participate, the classes were opened up to senior citizens from the village, with transport arranged. This study shows how the organisers adjusted the campaign to fit unexpected circumstances and benefited a wider audience as a result.

The Secretary of State for Education, launched Adult Learners' Week in Yorkshire at Meadowhall Shopping Centre. The launch featured demonstrations, music, celebrity appearances, and live interviews with adult learners. The event was filmed for Meadowhall Television and excerpts were broadcast at the Centre throughout the Week. Hundreds of enquiries were logged.

The Vauxhall Motors Employee Guidelines Centre in Luton set up stands in the factory for the Open University, colleges, library and guidance services. A presentation ceremony was held at the end of the Week for 140 employees who had finished courses in the last six months.

Surrey Adult Education staged a 'Lark in the Park' in Reigate's Priory Park. A whole programme of activities were staged including keep fit sessions, jazz dance, craft demonstrations and wildlife walk-abouts, while the careers service held CV clinics and ran help shops.

Dancing from 'dawn till dusk' was on offer to the people of Brixworth, Northamptonshire. Fourteen hours of free dance tuition took in the forms of flamenco, jazz, Latin American and tap dancing.

- exhibitions, competitions or quizzes;
- receptions, breakfasts or lunches;
- conferences or press conferences;
- journeys on public transport;
- meetings, discussions or debates;
- performances;
- launch of research findings.

Campaigners may find that the more simple the activity, the more effective it can be. Sometimes it is better to build on what you know works and develop it slowly. You will have to raise funds for the activity, so try to arrange something viable.

Activities should be relevant or appealing to the group you are trying to target. It's equally important to think about accessibility, timing, appropriateness of event, celebrities you may be able to involve, funding you will have to raise, staffing, health and safety issues, equipment and the space you will need.

Choose your venue

Many of the most successful events take place in venues that adults find accessible, friendly and familiar, such as cafés, bars, community centres, sports grounds, village halls or on public transport. You could even consider taking a 'learning bus' or mobile library into rural villages, housing estates or parks.

It's essential to pick a venue in which your audience will feel comfortable. But always pick one appropriate to the activity.

Think about:

- Where is the venue? Is it easily accessible for your participants?
- How big is it?
- Is there access for disabled people?
- What sort of staffing does it already offer, and will you have to arrange more?
- Is it heated or air-conditioned?
- Does it have toilets?
- Does it have first-aid facilities or trained staff?
- It is insured?
- Does it have electrical points, a kitchen or access to refreshments?
- Does it have crèche facilities?

Participants value informality and a relaxed atmosphere. Staff and volunteers need to be easily identifiable but informally dressed. There may be value in more obvious identifiers such as caps or t-shirts bearing a logo or special colour.

Making sure they know where they're going...

People attending your event will appreciate a helping hand as soon as they step inside. You could provide clear signposting to all available activities. Better still, position staff just inside the door to offer a welcoming smile and directions. Some participants need extra encouragement to 'give it a go'. Tutors or trained volunteers will offer encouragement. Having advice and guidance workers to hand will ensure a fast response to initial needs. Where possible, some form of refreshments should be made available.

All staff and volunteers need to be sensitive to the fact that some participants may have the need of basic skills support . There is also benefit in having trained basic skills tutors available to support specialists offering learning activities to talk with participants who may have basic skills support needs.

Things to build into your planning:

- set-up time;
- map of surrounding area;
- programmes;
- an identified person responsible or organiser;
- technical help from venue;
- signposting;
- crèche;
- supply of refreshments/food;
- volunteers;
- staff to engage with participants;
- information, advice and guidance available to give general support;
- handouts and things for people to take away;
- registration and evaluation;
- clearing up.

...not forgetting your staff:

- training for those attending the activity;
- sharing of roles and responsibilities;
- backup for staff who are ill;
- involvement of volunteers to signpost people to the event and venue.

...or what happens afterwards:

- paying bills;
- writing report of the day;
- thank you letters to participants and partners;
- evaluation of event;
- dissemination meeting;
- plans/recommendations for future events.

ASPIRATIONS

A pint and a prospectus please –
Airedale and Wharfedale College linked
with Tetley's to promote short courses
in pubs.

Cut, advice and blow dry –
Rycotewood College took advice
sessions to hairdressing salons.

In Liverpool, Mersey Ferries
resounded with poetry, reading,
drama and music of all kinds in a
boatload of learning.

Empty city centre shops were used in
Coventry for free workshops in arts
and crafts activities.

In Cheshire, Macclesfield
College worked with the
National Trust transforming disused
sandstone quarries into an inspira-
tional open-air sculpture
workshop.

9 Publicity

Research

When arranging publicity for a particular activity you need to consider the target group carefully and research what they are likely to see, read or hear on a daily basis.

The best promotional materials will focus on everyday issues that are important to people. They will adopt a tone of voice that is encouraging, rather than demoralising or condescending.

As part of our research at NIACE we asked learners to comment on the posters we produce for Adult Learner's Week. We found that:

- Words are the most important part of the message, and people prefer a clear and straightforward explanation of the learning benefits.
- Colour and graphics can draw people to look but the content must relate to the person looking at it for it to be read.
- Showing people in a learning activity is desirable as it exemplifies what others might wish to do. Showing real people is more realistic and convincing than using symbolised characters – provided people can see themselves or their situations exemplified. One learner said: *"This is showing childcare and single parents – it's obviously aiming at young mothers."*
- A direct appeal to what people can get out of learning is better than leaving it to people to work out the message. There is a balance to be struck, however, between too little content and too much. Two learners said: *"The tube ad is simpler and more straightforward. The bus ad tries to say too much."*

  "They are easily seen and read because there is nothing else to do on the tube and the bus. There is more information in these ads – a better message."

- Putting real people in the ad is a good idea providing different family arrangements can be shown. Two learners said: *"Learning is a family thing, so it is nice to feature families."*

  "I liked this one because it shows she has brought up a family and it says now is the time to learn."

The impact achieved when people can relate to the subject and see themselves mirrored in the picture should not be under-emphasised. Photographs need to reflect the full diversity of society in terms of race, class, age and gender as well as giving proper representation to people with disabilities. Problems arise when people feel excluded from the images represented in photographs and for this reason cartoons may have a broader appeal. If you have a choice, real pictures strike a chord and make people say, *"That's me – if they can do it, I can do it."*

Bookmarks giving information about events in Oxfordshire were inserted into every library book loaned out in Oxfordshire prior to the event.

In a venture believed at the time to be the first of its kind in the country, Adult Learners' Week was publicised in Bradford via its own radio station. The station, funded by Bradford and Ilkley Community College, broadcast 24 hours a day throughout the Week. Information on learning opportunities was mixed with interviews with adult learners and celebrities.

Two tickets to New York, donated by British Airways, was the prize offered by Cirencester College for a paper plane-making competition.

Shoppers in Hampshire received a 'check-out' leaflet at Sainsburys and Tesco Stores, in an initiative organised by Hampshire County Council.

Channel 4 printed more than 300,000 beer mats with a learning message which were distributed through more than 300 Courage pubs.

The media

The media includes all forms of mass communication including local and national newspapers, publications and magazines, video, film and television and the internet. One of the best ways of getting people to hear about your campaign is through the press and broadcast media.

The value of the press and broadcast media is that is they are popular and can provide effective and sophisticated ways to alert local communities to the existence of courses and opportunities, to the achievements of learners, and to the impact that learning can bring to their own lives.

Those who control and work the various media are always looking for good stories, or a local angle on a national story. If you do have a good story, follow some basic guidelines and you will find producers and editors more receptive than you thought.

- Decide what kind of story you have – is it advertising, news, features or listings?
- Ask yourself – is it something that local newspapers or local television would be interested in?
- Decide on your key message.
- Prepare the resources you have – they could include a local learner or local group.

The hardest thing often to decide is whether you've got news or a feature. News items are linked to specific dates, one-off events, new research findings or something which will be new to readers or listeners. The thing about news items is their immediacy – if it's not new, then it's not news.

If there's a point you want to get across and you have a good story, consider writing a feature. People relate to human interest stories and they make good reading. Such stories depend on having personal contact with the subject of your feature, but also with people who work in the media. You need to spend the time building up these contacts over time. Who do you know who would be interested in promoting your work? Who can you get to know who could be helpful? Share the question with colleagues and you might find someone with the contacts you need.

Some magazines have long lead-in times (many up to three months) so talk to the editor well in advance of your preferred publication date. Be warned that editors have no built-in chat time and will only consider your story if it relates to their readers and the subject of the magazine. You'll have only a few minutes to convince them!

Listings are just that – a list of forthcoming activities or events. You can easily promote your event, and at minimal cost, just by sending a short note to the relevant page (check out the newspaper or magazine for address details). Sometimes editors receiving a press release will turn it into a listing rather than a news item.

Advertising is different from editorial coverage and can be expensive. If you must advertise, always use clear, crisp text, and remember that visual items such as photos will catch the eye faster than long paragraphs of copy.

Some dos and don'ts:

- Identify all possible outlets for your story and remember that no outlet is too small. Free newspapers are often more widely read than national dailies.
- Familiarise yourself with local and national newspapers, weekly and monthly periodicals, trade press, free press, specialist disability and minority ethnic press, women's magazines, local radio and television programmes.
- Identify the contact name of the right person for your type of story. Look through your local paper for stories with themes similar to yours. Make a note of the section and the writer and try to place a similar story in the same section yourself.
- Call the local newspapers or radio stations and ask for the name of the most relevant person to your story, for example, the news editor, features editor, environment correspondent, or picture editor for photographs. When you know who to contact, try telephoning or writing to them directly.
- When you send a release you're entitled to follow it up with a phone call (the editor or producer might take the opportunity to delve into the story further) but don't harass them.
- Local television will sometimes cover stories during Adult Learners' Week, but don't contact them before you are properly prepared with all the facts.
- Be creative with your story. You will have more chance of success if you can make it interesting or unusual in some way. Identify whether your story is exclusive as this may affect the type of coverage it receives.
- Remember that once you have created your story you need to keep the momentum going, making sure that you are accessible at all times. Give your contact numbers so that you can be reached.
- Don't give up if your story doesn't get covered at first. Follow up your media contacts giving them ideas for new angles or slots. This will help you to build up a lasting relationship with them. Try to establish yourself with local media as the first port of call with whom journalists may want to consult again.

Timing

Establish a time frame – when do you want the coverage to happen? What media deadlines are involved? If you want to promote something, it's no good getting it covered after the event. If you want to disseminate or celebrate something, can you get the media involved on the day?

The value of images and film

Good-quality images can make all the difference to the readability of an article. Consider how a dry foreword can be livened up by placing a picture of the writer next to it. Or how photos of animals or babies attract the eye to the accompanying article. Pictures of adults actively engaged in their hobby or learning activity can be more interesting than a row of individuals holding certificates.

"Going back to learning got me a good job. I can now support my son and myself."

Mohamed
31
learner

© Richard Olivier

If you're thinking of using television, have some activity ready to be filmed, with cutaways to people confident enough to talk about their experiences.

Radio will work the same way – but without images to back up the talking. This means that everything you say will have to stand up on its own. Adults who have overcome hardship to return to learning can be very effective as models when their stories are broadcast on radio.

Things to watch out for

Not all publicity is good publicity. Many people's lives have been made a misery by the intrusion of the press and not all media workers have a public service remit. It's important to remember that you're trying to promote learning in the interests of learners. Your main responsibility is to them. Be sure that you and those you work

Ying
45
learner

"English is no longer a barrier. I can be a teacher again."

with, including learners, are well prepared for any encounters with the press. You can do this by:

- offering media training;
- building relationships with the journalists, editors or producers;
- writing briefing notes for the interviewee;
- talking it through with the person who is being interviewed.

The lowdown on press releases:

- Newsdesks have hundreds of releases landing on them every day. To stand out, yours has to be something extra special.

- Start the release with a short, catchy title giving a sense of the story in very few words (avoid puns – journalists will write their own).
- It is vital to keep the text short, to the point and newsworthy. Early on your release must cover five points: who, what, where, when and why.
- A journalist reading the first paragraph of a good press release needs to have the full story in the first paragraph.

Have a go yourself. Try writing 20 words on a piece of news you want the papers to cover. Then read the paragraph to someone else and ask them to tell you what the story is about. You don't have to get the five 'W's into the first paragraph, but ideally all of the essential information will become known within a few seconds of reading the release. Be careful though – the easiest way to lose a journalist's attention is to fill your first paragraph with acronyms, specialist words or jargon.

- Follow up the first paragraph with further information supported by a quote. The quote could add a new dimension to or reinforce the importance of the story. To add authority, name your source (but check with them first!) and give their job title.
- Make sure that you include in clear, bold print at the bottom of the document your contact details.
- Notes for editors should include details of your organisation and other related information to the body of the press release.

The technicalities

Use A4 letterhead, double-spacing, on one page, two at the most. Type 'Press Release' and the date in large print at the top. If you know it, include the name and title of the person for whose attention the release is intended.

The style throughout must be concise, journalistic, and as catchy and intriguing as possible. Make sure it is tempting enough for an editor deluged with press releases to follow up.

Checklist:

- identify your story and the media outlet;
- discuss what you want to do with colleagues and learners;
- identify a media representative in your organisation to field basic queries;
- identify experts who could answer more searching questions, or take part in an interview (look outside your organisation as well as within it);
- write a press release and follow it up;
- make sure you have the necessary photos, people for interview, case studies or research;
- be creative – but don't be manipulated.

Promotional material

Publicity materials can be distributed on or before your event to provide maximum attention and maximum coverage. Consider printed items, such as:

- leaflets;
- posters;
- newspaper supplements.

Consider advertising in or on:

- newspapers:
- periodicals:
- magazines;
- workplace payslips;
- trade press;
- in-store publications.

You'll need to consider whether it's necessary to translate into other languages, and how you're going to distribute what you produce. You can distribute through local stores, libraries, community centres and schools but also have volunteers who can distribute promotional material in different venues as well as talk to people to encourage them to participate. If budgets permit, it is useful to use several types of publicity because this broadens the range of participants you will reach. It is also important to offer an incentive for people who participate. You could offer a prize, food and drink, or the opportunity to meet a celebrity.

Posters are among the simplest ways of reaching people but there are potential pitfalls:

- if developing a poster then allowances need to be made for distribution and mailing costs;
- contact telephone numbers should be prominent;
- images and slogans must be acceptable to the 'field' of practice and other partners;
- where reading and writing skills of the target audience are negligible or absent, a poster will need to work visually.

If you are printing your own publicity materials there are one or two things you can do to keep costs down:

- print in one or two colours only;
- find out what methods are available and at what prices;
- plan how posters and leaflets are to be distributed, and how many you need;
- shop around for designers and printers, and always get estimates and quotes before you make any commitment.

"It's never too late to have faith in yourself and what you may achieve."

Fred
82
learner

Joana
38
learner

"I've improved my spoken English and seen more of the town I live in."

10 Sponsorship

Outstanding ideas need outstanding resources to support them. But funding your campaign isn't always about finding a multi-national company willing to part with hard cash.

Organisers can be creative in their fundraising attempts by finding partners to carry out events or offer in-kind support. Many Government-led initiatives offer grants, as do a variety of existing campaigns (Adult Learners' Week is just one of them). It's important to remember that money is only one of the resources needed – others include staffing, expertise, time and equipment.

Effective fundraising takes time and commitment. You need to know what you need the support for, how you're going to raise it, and from whom. A clear budget is essential.

What?

You should have clear proposals in place before you approach any potential sponsor. You need to communicate clearly what you are asking for and what your campaign will achieve. In place of money, you might find that companies are willing to 'lend' you staff who have a specific expertise (IT or PR skills, for example).

Companies may be more willing to help if approached for in-kind sponsorship rather than money, for example, shops may supply prizes for competitions, space may be offered to hold events and specialist shops might help with printing.

Who?

One very obvious source of funding is from existing partners. If a strong group has been built up, it should be possible to lever resources from the members. Consider tapping them for staffing needs, venues, printing, skills, new contacts or volunteers.

Support can be sought from local businesses. This is likely to be the most time-consuming element of your efforts, and you might find it helpful to take advice from someone who's done it before. Remember that you are not asking for something for nothing – if you have access to something which the business is trying to achieve through its corporate sponsorship department, then you are in a strong position to sell.

Some local companies you may wish to approach may include local printing businesses, media companies, banks or building societies, bookstores, residential colleges, supermarkets and shopping centres, nightclubs, hardware or DIY stores, garden centres or travel agencies.

When targeting the private sector, concentrate well on a few, rather than a lot indiscriminately, and research their interests. They may have supported similar initiatives in the past, or have interests in literacy, or improving the well-being of socially-disadvantaged groups.

How?

Whatever you are asking for, a professional approach is vital. Find out the name of the appropriate person and make your initial approach in writing followed by a phone call. After identifying your needs, arrange a meeting with a representative to outline the strategy and goals of your campaign.

© BARRY JOHNSON PHOTOGRAPHY

An unused portakabin was transformed into a learning facility for the employees on the Heanor Gate Industrial Park in Nottinghamshire. This innovative venture was a result of joint working between local students and the Heanor Gate businesses. Activities in the portakabin were targeted at workers who were reluctant learners – the accessibility and familiarity of the venue (along with the fact they'd helped build it) gave them a sense of confidence and motivated them to join in.

100,000 copies of the London Guide to Adult Learners' Week activities were published by Floodlight and were distributed through *Time Out* magazine. The guide listed hundreds of events run by colleges in and around London throughout the Week.

The Connex South East Dover-to-London line lent one compartment of a train to learning activities organised by Kent Adult Education Service.

Key points

- It's better to ask for money for specific items rather than for core administration costs. You could ask for support to cover the costs of producing promotional materials, or renting a hall for local events/award ceremonies, or holding a competition.
- TV companies might agree to sponsor local awards if they think it will make interesting viewing.
- If you have a theme, use it. Sportswear clubs or manufacturers may support in kind if you are helping adults learn through a sports or fitness theme, while various industries may agree to fund the production of literature on the benefits of gaining work-placed skills.
- Organisations may distribute materials for you to their clientele/employees or customers. The theme of learning can be interesting for everyone.

11 Evaluating the outcome

Thinking about appropriate methods of evaluation at the outset helps an organiser clarify aims and objectives, and tests if and how they have been achieved. You will have better evidence that the project has performed well and you will be able to generate ideas and tips that can be shared with others, to inform you for future years.

It should be a priority from the beginning of the project that the needs of the target group will be met by the activities you have in mind, and there should be an objective measure to tell if the activities have met those needs.

Evaluation needs to be built into project plans from the outset and should include:

- identifying performance indicators or success measures prior to the event;
- sharing evaluation methods/ideas with partners involved in the event;
- evaluating the key elements of the event, such as: award schemes, telephone helplines, research, involvement of national organisations, press cuttings, and media coverage;
- evaluating how any regional activities support any national initiatives.

Performance indicators might include:

- how many people took part;
- how many were unemployed, unskilled or retired;
- how much media attention and press coverage the festival gained.

You might also want to record qualitative information: was your publicity material helpful? Did adults attending the events feel they had gained something? Can you link the results to enrolments?

Keeping a record of articles in the press (newspapers, magazines, journals) or features on the TV or radio will contribute to the overall picture of success of your campaign.

Evaluation of publicity materials produced could include:

- numbers of leaflets distributed/taken away/ handed in at activities;
- number of telephone calls/enquiries generated by leaflets;

- focus groups on effectiveness of leaflets/posters motivating the target group – these could be held prior to the production of the materials;
- appropriateness of materials produced for the target group;
- tokens/vouchers handed in at enrolment times.

Involving learners

Evaluation presents another opportunity to involve existing learners. Learners can be asked to don the guise of the Mystery Shopper, attending events and observing their effectiveness – or otherwise.

Evaluation of this kind can give organisers an insight into elements of the event which are very difficult to measure – the 'feel' of the event, its usefulness, and any tips for improvement. If you decide to use the mystery shopper option, offer your shopper the guidelines of what you most want to understand. For example, you might want feedback on the suitability of the venue, the level of advice and guidance offered, next steps, helpfulness or efficiency of staff, food offered and general ambience.

Getting the best out of the evaluation

Use the information you have gathered to provide feedback to key players through:

- written reports or newsletters;
- bullet points on your website.

Understanding what didn't work is as important as understanding what did, and will help refine your work for future campaigns.

12 Check it out

Good practice:

- starts by not promoting or marketing what you can't deliver, so make sure that provision is there;
- ensures that good planning has taken place with research or consultation to find out what is being done already;
- encourages partnership working between local people and with other interested agencies to support, build and plan collaborative, relevant activities;
- relates to the wider social, cultural and economic context in which target audiences are situated as well as to learners' interests, concerns and aspirations;
- involves celebrating, signposting or supporting the learners into further opportunities according to their individual aims and objectives;
- highlights and supports the learners as promoters of adult learning;
- production and dissemination of relevant publicity material for the target audience using the most appropriate media channels;
- produces a final report based upon the monitoring, review and evaluation data gathered during the duration of the activity in order to develop and improve in future years.

Challenges:

- finding funding is always a challenge especially if it is longer-term funding;
- convincing the media that adult learning is 'sexy';
- reaching those adults who are the most difficult to reach and engaging them.

Glossary

Economically active refers to people who are in paid employment or contributing to the economy e.g. volunteers

Adult Learners' Week is a UK-wide motivational campaign which has at its core the aims of celebration, raising awareness of learning opportunities and trying to reach those adults who haven't had the chance to access adult learning opportunities. It was started in 1992 and is co-ordinated by NIACE, the National Institute of Adult Continuing Education

Taster sessions – type of activities which give participants the opportunity to 'try something new'.

Adult Learners' Forum – a meeting of adult learners currently involved in education who meet to offer support, share experiences and identify issues and concerns.

Mystery Shopper – someone who is anonymous who attends an activity and makes observations about it.

Further reading

Management of Voluntary Organisations: organising effective events, 1998, Karen Gilchrist, Croner Publications Ltd

Pandora's Box: Companion Papers on Motivation, Access and the Media, 1997, Naomi Sargant & Alan Tuckett, NIACE.

The Learning Festivals Guide, 2000, Francisca Martinez and Markus Weil, UNESCO/NIACE

Securing the right to learn, 2002, Fiona Aldridge, NIACE

Useful contacts and networks

Adult Basic Skills Strategy Unit
Level 1 Caxton House
Department for Education and Skills
Tothill Street
London SW1H 9HA
Tel: 020 7273 1223
Website: www.dfes.gov.uk/readwriteplus

BBC Education
White City
201 Wood Lane
London W12 7TS
Tel: 020 8752 5252
Email: edinf@bbc.co.uk
Website: www.bbc.co.uk

Channel 4 Television
124 Horseferry Road
London
SW1P 2TX
Tel: 020 7396 4444
Website: www.channel4.co.uk

Chartered Institute of Library and
Information Professionals (CILIP)
7 Ridgmount Street
London WC1E 7AE
Tel: 020 7255 0500
Fax: 020 7255 0501
Email: info@cilip.org.uk
Website: www.cilip.org.uk

Directory of Social Change
24 Stephenson Way
London
NW1 2DP
Tel: 020 7391 4800
Fax: 020 7391 4808
Email: info@dsc.org.uk

Independent Television Commission
33 Foley Street
London W1W 7TL
Tel: 020 7255 3000
Fax: 020 7306 7800
Website: www.itc.co.uk

Learning and Skills Council
Cheylesmore House
Quinton Road
Coventry
Cv1 2WT
Tel: 0845 0194170
Fax: 02476 493600
Email: info@lsc.gov.uk
Website: www.lsc.gov.uk

National Federation of Women's
Institutes
Denman College
Marcham
Abingdon
Oxfordshire OX13 6NW
Tel: 01865 391991
Fax: 01865 391966
Email: denman@nfwi-unit.org.uk
Website: www.nfwi.org.uk

Workers' Educational Association
Temple House
17 Victoria Park Square
London E2 9PB
Email: national@wea.org.uk
Website: www.wea.org.uk

Workplace Basic Skills Network
CSET
Cartmel College
Lancaster University
Lancaster LA1 4YL
Tel: 01524 593405
Fax: 01524 844788
Email: wbs.net@lancaster.ac.uk
Website: www.lancs.ac.uk/wbsnet

Useful websites

www.unesco.org/education/uie/International ALW/FestivalsWorld.htm

www.niace.org.uk/alw

www.lifelonglearning.dfes.gov.uk/calendar.htm

www.nottinghamcvs.co.uk/information/organising

www.lsc.gov.uk

www.dfes.gov.uk/readwriteplus

www.learndirect.co.uk

www.dfes.gov.uk/get-on/

www.ufi.com

www.bss.org

www.campaign-for-learning.org.uk